Materials

Graham Peacock

Thomson Learning • New York

Books in the series:

ASTRONOMY • ELECTRICITY • FORCES
HEAT • LIGHT • MATERIALS
SOUND • WATER

First published in the
United States in 1994 by
Thomson Learning
115 Fifth Avenue
New York, NY 10003

First published in Great Britain in 1994 by
Wayland (Publishers) Ltd.

Library of Congress Cataloging-in-Publication Data
Peacock, Graham.
   Materials / Graham Peacock.
      p.   cm. – (Science activities)
   Includes bibliographical references and index.
   ISBN: 1-56847-076-2
   1. Materials – Juvenile literature. [1. Materials –
Experiments. 2. Experiments.] I. Title. II. Series.
TA403.2.P33   1994
620.1'1'078 – dc20   93-51024

Printed in Italy

Acknowledgments
The publishers would like to thank the following for allowing their
pictures to be used in this book: NHPA 9; Science Photo
Library 6, 23.
All artwork is by Tony de Saulles.

Contents

Words that appear in **bold** are explained in the glossary on page 30.

Wood

Wood is a **solid** material. It has a fixed shape and size.

You will need:

♦ **different wooden objects, natural and manufactured**

All the materials we use were either taken out of the earth or came from a living thing. Sometimes these natural materials are used to make other manufactured materials.

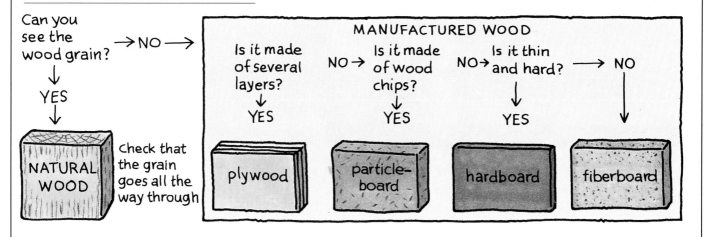

Can you see the wood grain? →NO→

↓

YES

↓

NATURAL WOOD

Check that the grain goes all the way through

MANUFACTURED WOOD

Is it made of several layers? NO→ Is it made of wood chips? NO→ Is it thin and hard? → NO

↓ YES   ↓ YES   ↓ YES   ↓

plywood   particle-board   hardboard   fiberboard

Make particleboard

You will need:

♦ sawdust ♦ glue ♦ wax paper

1 Mix the sawdust and glue together into a stiff paste.

2 Sprinkle sawdust on the wax paper, then spread the paste on top so that it is ¼ in. thick.

3 Let it set for a day or two.

4 Test the strength of your particleboard. How could you make it stronger?

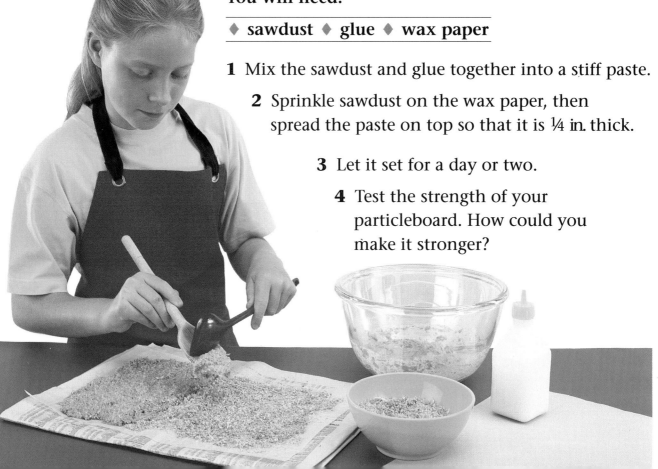

Good material for a floor?

You will need:

♦ pieces of balsa, particleboard, pine, plywood, or other wood ♦ screwdriver, dropper, and other simple tools ♦ container of water ♦ pencil ♦ paper

1 Think of ways to test the materials to see which would be best for flooring.

2 Carry out your tests. Which material would you use for flooring?

3 Now design a fair test to find the best material for a kitchen cutting board.

You will need an adult's help if you use a knife.

Floating wood

1 Collect different types of wood. (It is best if they have a similar shape.)

2 Predict which will float the best.

3 Put the pieces of wood into some water. Draw them from the side to show their positions in the water.

TESTING WOOD FOR A FLOOR

► Scratch with a screwdriver

► Spill colored water onto it

► Hit with a hammer

► Test for strength

1in. thick

a brick

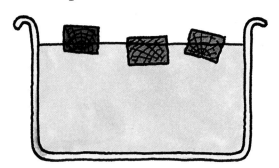

Did you know?

Lignum vitae is a wood used to make bowls. The wood is so **dense** that it sinks in water.

The biggest living tree is the sequoia tree that grows in California. You could make five billion matches from one tree!

Paper

What is paper made from?

You will need:

- ◆ tissue paper
- ◆ newspaper
- ◆ tape
- ◆ a magnifying glass
- ◆ a microscope

1 Carefully tear a damp sheet of tissue. Look through a magnifying glass at the fibers on the torn edge.

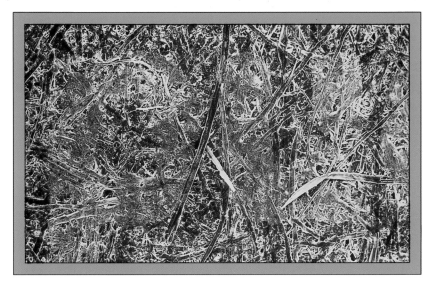

2 Stick a piece of tape onto a piece of newspaper. Rip it off. Look at the fibers on the tape through a microscope.

This highly magnified picture of newsprint shows clearly the fibers of wood. Newsprint is made by grinding logs between rough stones.

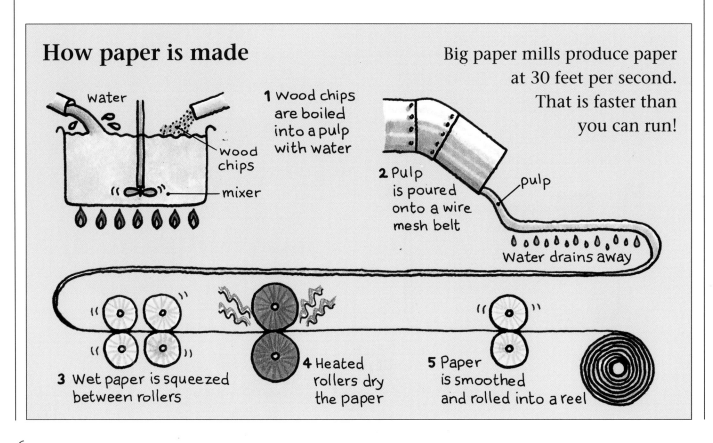

How paper is made

Big paper mills produce paper at 30 feet per second. That is faster than you can run!

water

wood chips

mixer

1 Wood chips are boiled into a pulp with water

2 Pulp is poured onto a wire mesh belt

pulp

Water drains away

3 Wet paper is squeezed between rollers

4 Heated rollers dry the paper

5 Paper is smoothed and rolled into a reel

How do you recycle paper?

You will need:

- tissue paper ◆ sieve ◆ newspaper
- a large pitcher ◆ a rolling pin
- 2 pieces of cloth (or clean paper)

1 Tear the tissue paper into shreds.

2 Mix the tissue with plenty of warm water to make a **pulp**.

3 Strain the pulp through a sieve.

4 On newspaper, lay a piece of cloth or clean paper . Spread the pulp on it.

5 Put the other piece of cloth and more newspaper on top. Using the rolling pin, squeeze out the water.

Find out:

- which type of paper makes the best recycled writing paper.

- if it helps to add a little wallpaper paste to the pulp.

Ancient paper

Before paper was invented, people made marks on soft clay tablets.

The Chinese invented the first real paper in A.D. 105.

Messy ink

Do not use newspaper for your recycled paper. The ink is very dirty and difficult to clean off your hands.

Testing paper

You will need:

- tissue paper
- newspaper
- a pencil-and-weight apparatus like the one below ◆ scissors

1 Carefully tear a sheet of tissue paper in one direction.

2 Now try to tear it in the other direction.

Why do you think that it tears more easily in one direction than in the other?

Find out:

- if newspaper tears more easily one way than the other.

Paper strength

1 Cut some paper into the shape shown opposite. Where does it always rip when you hold it up in the apparatus?

2 Set up the test for other kinds of paper. What kind of paper is the strongest? Is your test fair?

Find out:

- what weight a piece of paper that is ¼ in. wide at the neck will hold.

- if a piece of paper ½ in. wide at the neck will hold twice as much as one that is ¼ in. wide.

How strong is a tissue?

You will need:

- ◆ tissue paper ◆ a clean, safe can
- ◆ a plastic cup (smaller than the can)
- ◆ a rubber band ◆ assorted objects

1 Put dry tissue paper over the rim of the can. Secure it with a rubber band.

2 Stand the plastic cup on the tissue. Place small objects in the cup. How much weight will the tissue support?

3 Plan an experiment to find out how much wet tissue paper will support.

Make a papier mâché puppet
You will need:

- ◆ newspaper
- ◆ wallpaper paste

1 Tear some newspaper into strips.

2 Soak it in thin wallpaper paste.

3 Crumple dry newspaper into a ball.

4 Cover the ball with the wet newspaper. Let it dry.

5 Put another layer of strips over the ball. Shape a nose and chin from the **papier mâché**.

Natural papier mâché

Some wasps make nests from chewed paper and spit. The paper has colored layers showing where the wasps have used different woods.

Paper wasps make their nests from chewed-up wood.

9

Fabrics

How are fabrics made?

You will need:

♦ fabrics, including, felt, wool, printed cotton, and pantyhose
♦ a magnifying glass or microscope

Sort the **fabrics** into these four groups:

knitted

felt

Woven and printed

woven with colored thread

How are threads made?

You will need:

♦ a small cottonball

1 Very gently pull some fibers and twist them with your finger and thumb. (You could try rolling the cotton on your knee.)

2 Gently pull and twist until you have twisted a thread.

3 Notice that the twisted thread is much stronger than the loose fibers.

How are fibers dyed?

Warning! You must ask an adult to help with this activity.

You will need:

♦ natural juices for dyeing ♦ an old saucepan ♦ a pitcher
♦ a sieve ♦ salt ♦ 2 bowls ♦ white fabric or muslin

Note: *To obtain suitable juices for dyeing fabric, boil a vegetable or fruit that yields a colorful juice, such as spinach, red cabbage, blackberries, or even onion skins. Canned beet juice is also a good dye, but for this activity do not use beets packed in vinegar. Strain the juice through a sieve and cool before using.*

1 Pour the **liquid** into the bowls.

2 Add a spoonful of salt to one of the bowls.

3 Put a piece of fabric into each bowl. Let it soak for about 3 hours.

4 Take out the dyed fabric and let it dry. Did the salt help the fabric to take the dye?

Did you know?

The red **dye** cochineal, which is used for fabrics, food, and lipstick, comes from the boiled and crushed bodies of small insects. The insects live on cacti in Mexico and Central America.

Plastics

You will need:

1 Gently pull each strip.

2 What do you notice happening as they begin to stretch?

3 Keep stretching each strip until it is about to snap.

4 Place all the stretched plastic strips in line on a piece of paper.

Which plastic strip stretched the most?

Changed plastic

Take the plastic strip that stretched the most. What do you think will happen if you try to stretch it again?

Is paper as strong as plastic?

To find out, use material from paper and plastic bags in a fair test. You might want to use the apparatus from page 8.

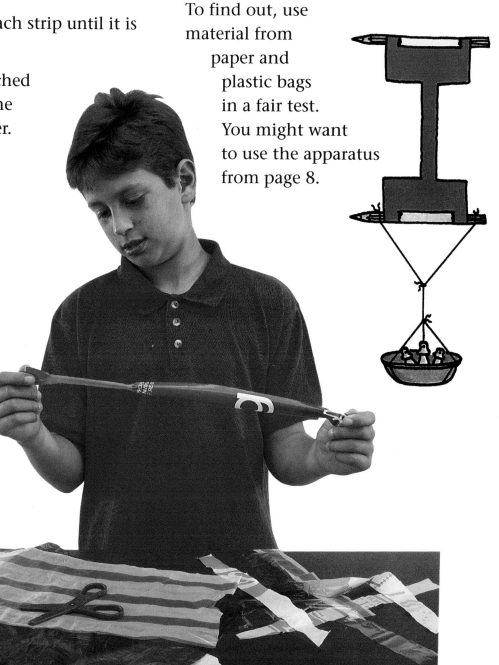

12

Is plastic or paper best for wall covering?

You will need:

♦ samples of wall coverings, including paper and **vinyl** ♦ a hammer ♦ oil ♦ sandpaper ♦ water ♦ scissors ♦ kitchen cleanser

1 List some ways to test for the best kitchen wall covering.

2 Perform your tests and display your results.

3 Which covering would be best in a kitchen? Would you also choose it for a bedroom?

Where does it come from?

Plastic is a manufactured material. Most plastic is made from **petroleum**. Other petroleum products include rubber, detergents, cosmetics, and nylon.

Warm plastic

Plan tests to see if there are differences between warm and cold plastic. Here is an example:

	From the freezer	Room temp.	On the radiator
Strip of plastic bag	stretched 6 in.	stretched 7 in.	stretched 8 in.
Plastic adhesive	it feels hard	it feels stretchy	it feels soft

Warning!

Never burn or heat plastic in an oven!

Metals

Are all metals magnetic?

You will need:

♦ different metals, including steel and aluminum ♦ a magnet

Test each metal to see if it is attracted to the magnet.

Did you know?

Cassette tapes are coated with tiny particles of iron. The recording head magnetizes the particles into a code. The playback head reads the code and turns it into electrical signals that are fed to the speakers.

Are all metals very hard?

You will need:

♦ aluminum cans, steel cans, old cutlery, a nail (iron), a screw (steel), a piece of copper pipe, or other metal scraps

1 Use the nail to scratch different metals.

2 How deep does the scratch go into the metal?

3 Put the pieces of metal in order:

softest   hardest

Did you know?

Some metals, like sodium and potassium, are soft enough to be cut with a plastic knife.

14

Do all metals rust?

You will need:

♦ **different scrap metal pieces (include a steel can and an aluminum can – use a magnet to tell the difference)**

1 Scratch each object with a screw or nail.

2 Leave the cans and the other metal samples in a damp place for two days. Which are rusty? Where does the steel rust?

Tin can?

Steel cans are coated with tin. Tin will not rust, but it is soft so it is easily scratched off.

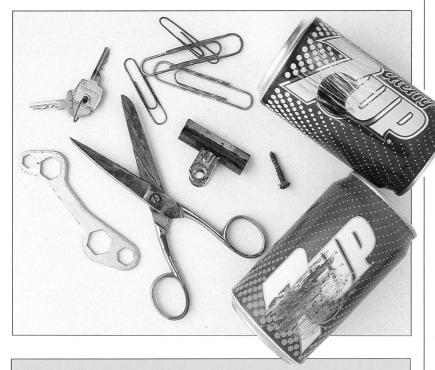

Did you know?

Aluminum is a light metal, so it is often used to make airplanes. If planes were made of steel or iron, they would be three times as heavy!

Do all metals weigh the same?

You will need:

♦ **samples of different metals**

Pick up the pieces of metal. Which ones feel heavy for their size? Which feel light for their size?

A 1 in. cube of aluminium weighs 1.5 ounces.

A block of gold the same size weighs 11 ounces.

A 1 in. cube of osmium metal weighs 13 ounces.

Mixing materials

Making concrete

You will need:

♦ 1 lb. cement ♦ 1 lb. sand ♦ 5 or 6 small boxes ♦ 3 spoons ♦ water ♦ an old bucket ♦ plastic sheet

---

1 Cover a table with the plastic sheet.

2 Measure out 6 spoonfuls of sand and 6 spoonfuls of cement. Mix them together carefully in the old bucket. Add enough water to make a thick mixture.

3 Pour your mixture into a box.

4 Make other concrete mixtures using different amounts of sand and cement and pour each into the other boxes.

5 Let the bars dry for a day.

Warning! Try not to touch the cement. Wash any splashes off your hands with clean water. Protect your eyes.

Test

Which mixture of concrete and sand makes the strongest bars?

Why do apples turn brown?

You will need:

- ♦ red or green apple ♦ sugar
- ♦ lemon juice ♦ water ♦ knife
- ♦ plastic bag

1 Carefully cut a slice from the apple.

2 Leave the slice in the open air for one hour. What changes do you notice?

3 Come up with an experiment to see if you can stop the apple slices from turning brown.

You could:
- put the slice in a bag.
- squeeze lemon juice on it.
- sprinkle sugar on it.

Oxidation

Apples turn brown because they combine with oxygen in the air.

Hot mixture

You will need:

- ♦ plaster of paris ♦ modeling clay
- ♦ a key, leaf, or other small object

1 Make a mold with the clay.

2 Press an object into the bottom of the mold. Take it out.

3 Mix some plaster of paris with water until the mixture is like thick cream.

4 Pour the plaster into the mold and leave it for 30 minutes. Feel the mold as the plaster sets.

Chemical reaction

Plaster of paris gets hot as it sets. This is because it reacts with the water and releases energy as heat. Design an experiment to see if plaster of paris will set even if the air cannot reach it to dry it out.

Mixtures

You will need:

- a dry mixture of lentils and beans
- 3 bowls ◆ a foil dish ◆ a sharp pencil ◆ a stopwatch

1 Time how long it takes to separate the beans and lentils using:

- your right hand.
- your left hand.
- both hands.

2 Push the pencil through the foil dish in several places to make a sieve. Push it through just enough to make small holes for the lentils to fall through.

How quickly can you sort the lentil and bean mixture now?

Sift whole-wheat flour

bran is left in sieve

small particles of flour go through

Money sorter

Can you make a money sorter that works like a sieve?

How can you separate mixtures?

You will need:

- a mixture of sand and salt
- a pitcher ◆ a funnel
- warm water ◆ filter paper
or absorbent paper towel

1 To separate the mixture of salt and sand, add warm water and stir.

What is **dissolved?**

What stays on the bottom?

2 Pour the water through the **filter**.

What gets caught in the paper?

3 Leave the solution of salty water to **evaporate**.

Mastering mixtures

Challenge your friends to separate mixtures of such things as:

chips of wax crayon (floats)
tiny staples (magnetic)
sand (not **soluble**)
salt (soluble)
marbles (too big to sift)
sugar (soluble)

Think of your own mixtures and how to separate them.

Salt production

Salt deposits were laid down millions of years ago. They used to be mined like coal. Most salt is now produced by dissolving the salt under ground.

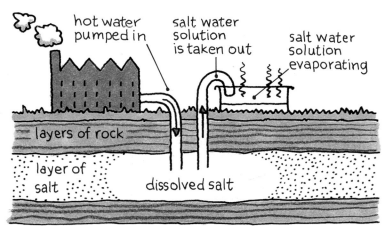

Solid to liquid

What changes happen as a candle burns?

Warning! You will need an adult to help you with these activities.

You will need:

- ◆ **2 small candles or tealights**
- ◆ **tray of sand** ◆ **matches**
- ◆ **small foil dish**
- ◆ **pieces of wax and crayons**

1 Handle a piece of wax for a few minutes.

What happens as it warms up in your fingers?

2 Stand one candle in the tray of sand. Light the candle.

3 What happens when liquid wax runs down the candle?

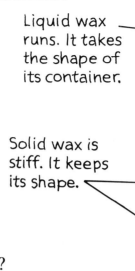

Liquid wax runs. It takes the shape of its container.

Solid wax is stiff. It keeps its shape.

Make your own candle

1 Put the other candle in the foil dish.

2 Place a few pieces of broken wax and colored wax crayons around the candle.

3 Light the candle. Let it burn until all the wax is melted.

4 Blow it out. When it is cool, remove the new candle from its mold.

Watch solids change when making oat squares

Warning! Ask for adult help when you are cooking.

You will need:

- ⅓ cup margarine ◆ baking pan
- 2 tablespoons sugar ◆ pan
- 2 tablespoons honey
- 2 cups rolled oats ◆ spoon
- chocolate (optional)

1 Gently heat the margarine, honey, and sugar in a pan until the two solids become liquid.

2 Mix the liquid with the oats. Press the mixture into a baking pan.

3 Bake at 375° F for 30 minutes.

4 Melt some chocolate to cover the cooled oat squares.

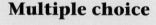

Multiple choice

1 The biggest living tree is a...
a) pine tree b) sequoia tree c) weeping willow

2 Which animals make their nests from chewed wood?
a) wasps b) bees c) beetles

3 The dye cochineal is made from...
a) crushed conch shells b) insects c) chemicals

4 Which of these is not manufactured?
a) nylon b) wool c) paint

5 Gold is how many times heavier than aluminum?
a) twice as heavy b) about five times as heavy
c) about seven times as heavy

Find the answers you are not sure of by looking back through this book. The answers are also given on page 32.

Liquids

Are some liquids runnier than others?

You will need:

- water ◆ wallpaper paste
- cooking oil ◆ 3 jars with lids ◆ 3 marbles or coins

1 Fill each jar with a different liquid.

Put a marble in each jar and screw on the lid.

2 Turn the jars over, all at the same time. (You will need help.)

Which marble falls the quickest?

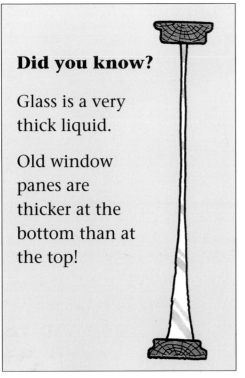

Did you know?

Glass is a very thick liquid.

Old window panes are thicker at the bottom than at the top!

Liquid race

You will need:

- ◆ dishwashing liquid, liquid soap, syrup, water, shampoo, oil, or other liquids ◆ an eye dropper ◆ tray

Put a drop of each liquid on a tray.

Tilt the tray.

Which liquid runs down most quickly?

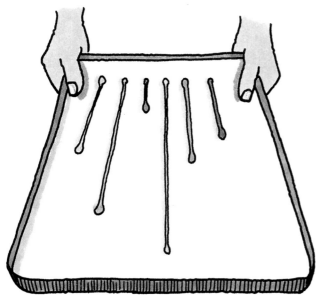

Are some liquids heavier than others?

You will need:

- ♦ cooking oil ♦ water ♦ a funnel
- ♦ colored cold salt water ♦ a clear jar
- ♦ plastic tubing to fit the funnel

1 Pour some water into the jar.

2 Using the tube, carefully pour the colored salt water underneath the tap water.

3 Gently pour the oil down the side of the jar, on top of the tap water.

4 Leave the jar for a week.

What changes do you notice?

Liquid metal

Mercury is a metal. It is a liquid at room temperature and freezes at -38° F. Mercury is used in thermometers. It used to be called quicksilver.

These shiny drops of the liquid metal mercury are very poisonous to humans. Mercury is so dense that even iron will float on it.

Acids and alkalis

Can tea be used as an indicator?

Warning! Do not use strong acids or strong alkalis like bleach for this activity.

You will need:

- ◆ a pot of cool tea ◆ 3 glasses
- ◆ white wine vinegar or lemon juice (acids) ◆ sodium bicarbonate, baking powder, or soap powder (alkalis) ◆ 3 teaspoons

1 Divide the cool tea among the glasses.

2 Add 2 teaspoons of vinegar to one glass. Add 1 teaspoon of baking powder to another glass.

3 Compare the colors with the tea in the third glass.

Experiment

Do you think you can change the color of the vinegar and tea mixture by adding small amounts of sodium bicarbonate to it? Try it and see.

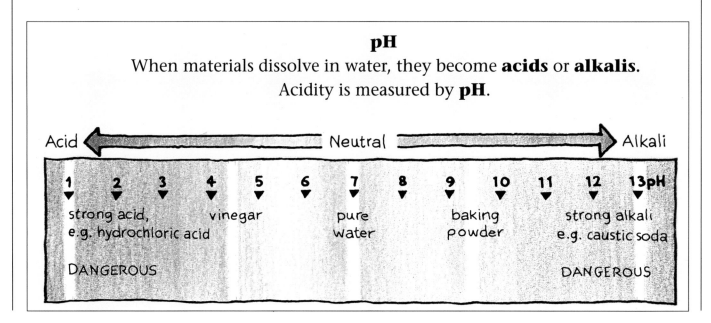

pH

When materials dissolve in water, they become **acids** or **alkalis**.
Acidity is measured by **pH**.

Acid ⟵ Neutral Alkali ⟶

1 2 3 4 5 6 7 8 9 10 11 12 13pH

strong acid, e.g. hydrochloric acid   vinegar   pure water   baking powder   strong alkali e.g. caustic soda

DANGEROUS   DANGEROUS

Cabbage color

You will need:

- fresh, chopped red cabbage
- warm water ♦ 2 pitchers ♦ a sieve
- glasses ♦ a variety of safe foods and household cleaners (do not use bleach or bathroom cleaners) ♦ a spoon

1. In a pitcher, soak the red cabbage in warm water. Squash it with a spoon or potato masher.

2. Strain the cabbage water into another pitcher. Pour it into several glasses.

3. Add drops of vinegar to one glass. Stir a little sodium bicarbonate or dish-washing liquid into another. This will show you acid and alkaline colors.

4. Add drops of other substances to clean cabbage water.

5. Make a list of your results.

Indicator paper

The best indicator paper is **universal indicator**.

You can make your own cabbage indicator paper by soaking blotting paper in a strong cabbage **solution**. Let it dry. Then cut up the paper. Dip it into different solutions. If the paper turns blue, the solution is an alkali. If it turns red, the solution is an acid.

Liquid to gas

Which is the best way to dry laundry?

You will need:

◆ **paper towels** ◆ **an eye dropper**

1 Use the eye dropper to dampen the paper towels. Hang them up to dry.

2 Check the towels often to see which dries first.

Crisp bread

Plan a test to find out where slices of bread get stale most quickly. Plan another test to discover how best to keep bread fresh.

Container evaporation

Test the idea that water evaporates faster from a bowl than from a bottle.

How will you make the test fair?

Water vapor

When water evaporates, it changes from a liquid to an invisible **gas**.

With an adult, watch a boiling teakettle.

DANGER! Steam can badly scald you

Steam evaporates to form invisible water vapor in the air

steam is formed by tiny drops of liquid water

invisible water vapor

Gas to liquid

Why do mirrors and windows steam up?

You will need:

◆ a glass that has been cooled
in the refrigerator
◆ a glass at room temperature

Take the glass out of the refrigerator.
Breathe on it. What do you notice?

Breathe on the warm glass. Compare the
results.

Water vapor in your warm breath is
cooled when it touches the cold glass.
This changes the vapor from a gas to a
liquid, which appears as droplets of
condensation.

Condensation
The water vapor in your breath
condenses in cold air.

Gas ➤ liquid ➤ solid

1 Stand a clean, safe can on a plate.

2 Fill it with ice and add lots of salt.
Notice the water condensing on
the outside of the can.

3 Eventually the ice and salt
mixture will become so cold that
it **freezes** the condensation on
the outside of the can.

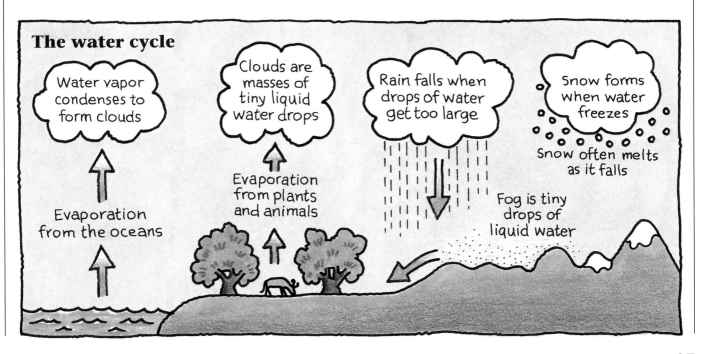

The water cycle

Water vapor condenses to form clouds

Clouds are masses of tiny liquid water drops

Rain falls when drops of water get too large

Snow forms when water freezes

Snow often melts as it falls

Evaporation from the oceans

Evaporation from plants and animals

Fog is tiny drops of liquid water

Gases

How is carbon dioxide produced?

You will need:

- ◆ a bottle ◆ a balloon
- ◆ bicarbonate of soda
- ◆ vinegar ◆ raisins
- ◆ 2 jars ◆ active dry yeast
- ◆ birthday cake candle
- ◆ modeling clay ◆ match

1 Put ½ teaspoon of bicarbonate of soda into the balloon.

2 Put 2 tablespoons of vinegar in the bottle.

3 Fit the balloon over the bottle's neck. Lift up the balloon so the powder falls into the vinegar.

4 Watch the balloon.

Rising raisins

1 Put a few raisins in a jar with yeast and water. (Do not use "rapid rise" yeast.)

2 Can you explain what happens?

Yeast feeds on the sugar in the raisins. It produces the gas **carbon dioxide**.

Fire extinguisher

1 Secure a birthday cake candle in a jar with some modeling clay.

2 Put 2 teaspoons of bicarbonate of soda into the jar.

3 Light the candle.

4 Dribble some vinegar carefully down the inside of the jar.

5 What happens to the candle?

carbon dioxide gas

dribble in vinegar

candle

jar

clay

bicarbonate of soda

Dissolving gas

Fizzy drinks – sodas – get their sparkle from carbon dioxide.

1 Empty a carbonated soft drink bottle.

2 Fill it about ¼ full with cold water.

3 Shake the bottle.

4 Explain what happens.

How could you test to see if the effect was really due to the remaining carbon dioxide?

Shrinking air

Put a closed, empty plastic drink bottle in the refrigerator or freezer. Predict whether the how the plastic bottle will change in the cold.

What do you think will happen when it warms up again?

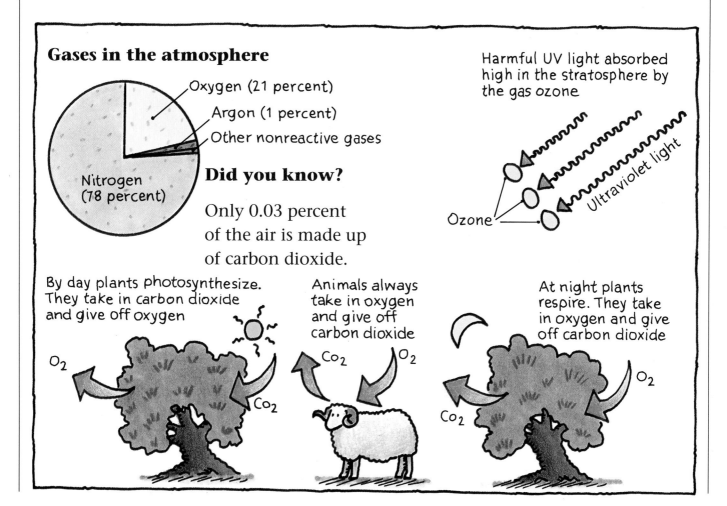

Gases in the atmosphere

Oxygen (21 percent)
Argon (1 percent)
Other nonreactive gases
Nitrogen (78 percent)

Did you know?

Only 0.03 percent of the air is made up of carbon dioxide.

Harmful UV light absorbed high in the stratosphere by the gas ozone

Ultraviolet light

Ozone

By day plants photosynthesize. They take in carbon dioxide and give off oxygen

O_2 Co_2

Animals always take in oxygen and give off carbon dioxide

Co_2 O_2

At night plants respire. They take in oxygen and give off carbon dioxide

O_2 Co_2

Glossary

Acids Solutions with many free hydrogen particles.

Alkalis Solutions with many free hydroxide particles (a mixture of hydrogen and oxygen).

Carbon dioxide A gas made of carbon and oxygen. Carbon dioxide makes up only 0.03 percent of the air.

Condensation Process through which a gas is changed into a liquid (often droplets).

Dense Having very tightly packed particles.

Dissolved When particles have become evenly spaced out in a liquid.

Dye A substance that colors other materials.

Evaporate To change from a liquid to a gas.

Fabrics Materials made from woven, knitted, or pressed fibers.

Filter A device for separating mixtures.

Freezes Changes from a liquid to a solid.

Gas A material, like air, that spreads out to fill any container and has no fixed size or shape.

Hardboard Sheets of hard material made from wood dust and resin squashed together under great pressure.

Indicator A material that shows whether a solution is acid or alkaline.

Lignum vitae A very dense tropical hardwood.

Liquid A material, like water, that flows and takes the shape of a container, but has a fixed size.

Oxidation The process in which a substance combines with the gas oxygen. Rust is oxidized iron.

Papier mâché A mixture of torn paper and glue.

Petroleum One of the products made when crude oil is refined.

pH The measure of acidity of a solution.

Pulp A mixture of wood fibers and water.

Solid A material that has a fixed size and shape.

Soluble Able to dissolve in a liquid.

Solution A mixture of a solid and liquid in which the molecules of the solid are evenly spaced out in the liquid. If a solid is dissolved, it will never settle out of the solution unless some of the liquid evaporates.

Universal indicator An indicator that measures the strength of an acid or an alkali.

Vinyl A type of plastic often made into sheets for wall and floor covering.

Water vapor Water that has evaporated to become a gas.

Books to read

Challand, Helen J. *Experiments with Chemistry.* Experiments. Chicago: Childrens Press, 1988.

Dyson, Susan. *Wood.* Resources. New York: Thomson Learning, 1993.

Jennings, Terry. *Materials.* The Young Scientist Investigates. Chicago: Childrens Press, 1989.

Laithwaite, Eric. *Using Materials.* Science at Work. New York: Franklin Watts, 1991.

Langley, Andrew. *Paper.* Resources. New York: Thomson Learning, 1993.

Peacock, Graham and Chambers, Cally. *The Super Science Book of Materials.* Super Science. Thomson Learning, 1993.

Richards, Roy. *101 Science Tricks: Fun Experiments with Everyday Materials.* New York: Sterling Publishing Co., 1991.

Chapter notes

Pages 4-5   Plan out the tests for flooring before you do them.

The way in which the blocks of wood float depends on the density of the wood. Balsa has a very low density and will float high on the water. Whether the blocks float flat on a face or diagonally on a corner depends on the center of gravity of the block.

Pages 6-7   Commercial paper recyclers use special processes to remove the ink from newsprint. Poor quality recycled paper is used to make gray cardboard.

Devise your own test for the best recycled writing paper. If you are short of ideas, watch how ink soaks into the recycled paper.

Pages 8-9   The fibers in most tissue paper are strongly aligned, which gives the paper a grain in one direction. The strength of a piece of paper depends on its width. Twice the width gives twice the strength, and so on. The length of the sample doesn't really matter. Paper is surprisingly strong, so make the samples as narrow as possible.

Pages 10-11   The cottonball is very weak before the fibers are twisted together. Friction is the force that keeps the fibers from sliding past each other, making the thread strong.

Pages 12-13   Another interesting plastic to test is the packaging that holds groups of cans together. It forms a neck fairly easily and continues to stretch under a relatively small force. Once the plastic has been stretched, it has little strength and the neck will snap very easily.

Pages 14-15   The only magnetic metals you are likely to encounter are iron and steel. Aluminum is much softer than steel.

When kept damp, iron and steel will both rust. Copper will develop a green coating called verdigris, which is either copper acetate or copper carbonate.

Pages 16-17   Concrete is not especially dangerous, but it can irritate the skin of some people. Wear an apron to protect your clothing. Other materials that oxidize include potatoes and wine.

Pages 18-19   If you find it difficult to obtain rock salt, simply mix the sand and salt together. When filtering, use a coffee filter if this is more convenient than a funnel and paper cone.

Pages 20-21   Always clear the table when working with candles. Tie back loose hair and clothing. Always ask an adult to help with candles and matches.

When making your own candle, notice that the liquid wax takes the shape of its container.

Pages 22-23   The thickness of liquids is measured by viscosity. Liquids become less viscous as they warm up. You could put identical blobs of liquid on two trays and compare them after one has been in the refrigerator for an hour and one left at room temperature.

Pages 24-25   The concept of acids and alkalis is complicated, so take time to explore the effects and color changes rather than worrying about the underlying chemistry. An acid will neutralize an alkali and vice versa.

Pages 26-27   Some people might think that the condensation on the outside of a cold can comes from inside the can. The cold, empty glass will help make it clear that condensation comes from the air around the can.

When you open the freezer door, you will often see water vapor from the air condense into a cloud of tiny droplets as it is suddenly cooled by the air from the freezer.

Pages 28-29   The raisins bob up and down in the jar as they are buoyed up by the carbon dioxide gas, then fall back to the bottom when the gas bubbles float away. There will still be some carbon dioxide, which is highly soluble, left in the soda bottle. The bottle will collapse as the gas dissolves. The water that results will taste like flat soda water.

Index

Answers to questions on page 21:
1 b, **2** a, **3** b, **4** b, **5** c